The

BOGAN

BB

BIBLE

First published 2017 in Macmillan by Pan Macmillan Australia Pty Ltd
1 Market Street, Sydney, New South Wales, Australia 2000

A CIP catalogue record for this book is available from the National Library of Australia: http://catalogue.nla.gov.au

Internal design and illustrations by Gino Campagnaro © asthetico design
Internal photography by Tony Mott and Pauly Fenech © Housos, Stolen and Antichocko Productions

Images on pp i–iii, 6-7, 8, 10, 12, 14, 16, 18, 19, 20, 22, 24, 26, 34, 35, 46-51, 53 (drug-related belly), 61 (babies), 67, 69, 71, 73, 79 (trophies), 86-90 (background), 91, 92-93 (background), 95, 97, 101, 103 (background), 111, 113, 115: iStock
Images on pp 29, 52 (tattooed belly), 53 (pregnant and pierced belly), 54, 55 (signpost), 61 (woman), 75, 77, 80-81 (map background), 99, 103: Shutterstock
Photo of Peter Brock on p9: AAP Image/Mark Horsburgh
Photo of Bon Scott on p13: Pictorial Press Ltd/Alamy Stock Photo
Image on p31: ShotbyShane
Images on p37 (clockwise from left): Getty Images Sport/Getty Images; David Redfern/Getty; Julian Parker/Getty Images
Image on p38: Bentley Archive/Popperfoto/Getty Images
Photo of Kath & Kim on p56: Everett Collection Inc/Alamy Stock Photo
Images on p80 (clockwise from left): Rob Walls/Alamy Stock Photo; Ingo Oeland/Alamy Stock Photo; Mike Greenslade/Australia/Alamy Stock Photo
Image on p85: Wes Boyd
Image on p107 taken from the television series *Upper Middle Bogan* - Gristmill/ABC TV
Image on p109 (Earth): Purestock
Image on p116: Fin Costello/Redferns/Getty
Image on p126 © Alex Stitt for Recreation Australia Limited and 'Life. Be in it.' International Pty Ltd.

Printed by McPherson's Printing Group

The BOGAN

BB

BIBLE

Pauly Fenech

MACMILLAN

From the Author

Hello Bogans, Bogan enthusiasts and the yet-to-be-convinced-of-their-Boganicity.

If you don't know me my name is Pauly Fenech. I am the foremost Boganologist in the world.

Many years spent travelling far and wide during my career in entertainment have introduced me to all manner of subcultures in the beautiful country we call Australia. But I have seen an insidious change taking hold. The forces of political correctness are sweeping this sunburnt land. The attitudes and sense of humour that were once considered 'Aussie' are now under fire.

As Australia becomes more and more Americanised, we are losing the soul that has made us famous worldwide as a nation like no other.

There is one last hope. **THE BOGAN.**

VEGEMITE

CONCENTRATED YEAST EXTRACT

KRAFT

WHAT ARE BOGANS?

Bogans are top-shelf, black-label, gold-class Aussies. They embody all the great aspects of our proud culture — mateship, humour, love of sport and socialising, and the ability to drink anyone under the table.

Bogans may be the last line of defence of the Digger spirit being eroded by the elites who scoff at this noble breed of Australian. They use the term Bogan as an insult. But to be labelled a Bogan is actually a great compliment. Bogans are carefree, individual, wild, loyal, honest, humorous people who live fast and with passion.

Many of you reading this Bible are definitely Bogans in denial. Now is the time to embrace your Boganicity. To support your Bogans. To cherish and love your Bogans. This Bogan Bible will show you how.

Pauly Fenech

Contents

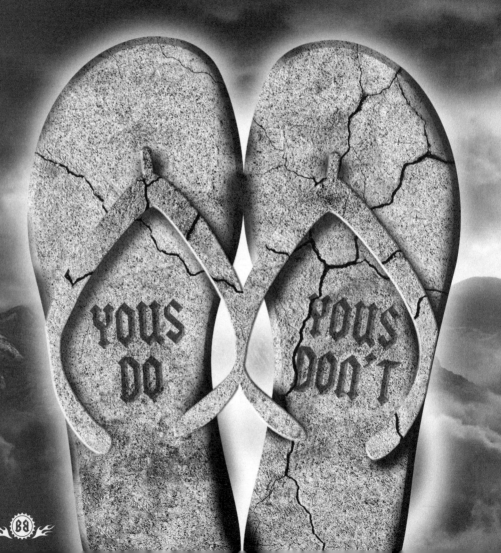

The BOGAN 10 COMMANDMENTS

1 Yous shalt have no driver before Brock.

In the Bogan world there is only one iconic racing champion: Peter Brock. Raised on the family diet of Vegemite mixed into mashed potatoes, Brocky was in the army when he first sucked in sweet diesel fumes at Bathurst. He went on to become the racing driver of every Bogan's dreams. Although 'Big' Dick Johnson ran a close second, Brock – with nine Bathurst 1000 wins, another nine Sandown 500 victories, and almost 40 years in the Holden colours – was the ultimate V8 god. Sadly, Brocky didn't survive his final prang in 2006 but he has lived on in every Bogan burnout since.

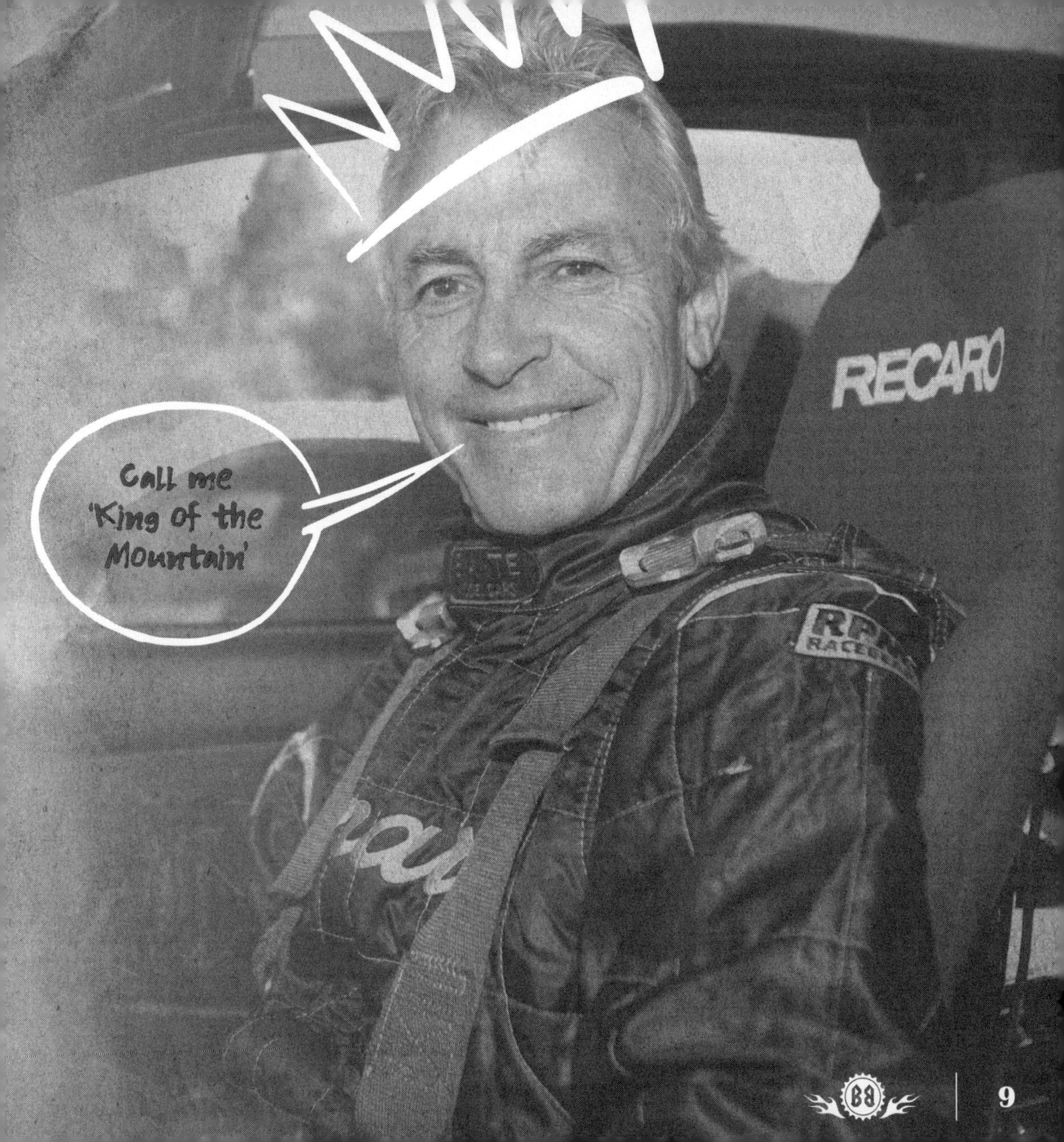
Call me 'King of the Mountain'
RECARO

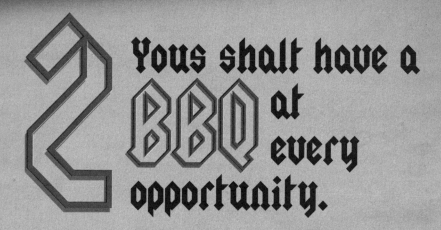

2 Yous shalt have a BBQ at every opportunity.

The ritual burning of flesh has its origins in the pagan
world and Bogans also commit to this rite of passage
on public holidays, birthday parties, family reunions,
weekends and weekdays. Like the Viking tradition of
burning fallen heroes on boats, the barbie is a sacred
ritual of great cultural significance.
Gentleman Bogans bring the meat and beer.
Lady Bogans bring the bread and Cruisers. And the kids.

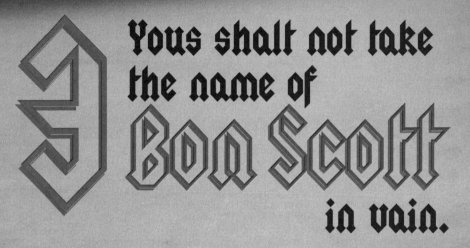

Yous shalt not take the name of Bon Scott in vain.

Another god of the Bogan world is Ronald 'Bon' Scott.
Although AC/DC successfully reformed with a new singer after
Bon's death from acute alcohol poisoning in 1980, Bogan elders
still treasure the Aussie band's original frontman. His rude,
crude, tattooed charm and cunning linguist ways with lyrics
made him one of the foremost inspirations for Bogan attitude
and musical excellence.

4 Remember thy weekend. Yous shalt Party.

The importance of blowing off steam on Friday and Saturday nights must be upheld. Without the weekend to look forward to, existence is meaningless in Bogan life.
Traditional Bogan ceremonies on the weekend include nudie runs, watching footy, doing burnouts and, of course, having barbies.

5 Honour thy parents. If in doubt get an AVO.

Whether related by birth or marriage or de facto, all Bogans (when sober) have a healthy respect for their parents. If disrespected, a Bogan parent will freely banish a young Bogan from the house. Nannas who party get much respect. The older the Nan and the more she parties, the higher her status in Bogan society.

The Bogan Pop, however, isn't afforded the same respect as Bogan Nan. Instead Bogan Pop is expected to play Tong-master at BBQs, hold the remote control during sports fixtures and tinker with pet projects like restoring an old Holden or Ford to its former glory. Or work.

6 Yous shalt not be a Wanker.

Confidence is one thing, but in the Bogan world showy acts or bragging behaviour is frowned on. Bogans like a quiet achiever (unless they are drunk and then a loud, silly achievement can be celebrated). Examples of 'Wanker acts' in the Bogan world include: Big-noting yourself • Name-dropping sports figures as mates (i.e. bullshitting) • Overdressing for any occasion • Becoming vegan • Voting for the Greens • Being a hipster • Being a constant smart-ass.

Chip on shoulder

Common Wanker phrases:

'Is this snag organic?'

'Just heading off to me mindfulness class #blessed'

'I was having a beer with me mate Warnie...'

Italian Suit over $500

Big name watch brand

7 attitude
is everything.

What is the Bogan attitude? Bogans are generous and genetically happy creatures. But when challenged, the Bogan has both bark and bite. So if you survey a group of Bogans in their natural setting and ask their attitude to life, their reply will boil down to: 'I don't care what other people think of me'.

8 Yous shalt not steal.

Pinching from Wankers is allowed. But not your mates.
Note: this commandment can be bent (never broken) in Bogan
relationships. While it's always considered bad form to root your
mate's other half, it's not unusual for Bogan partners to switch
around. However, before this happens there must be a cooling-off
period for both men and women. Otherwise there will be a social
media barrage between the ladies and a possible 'flogging' or
'punch on' might eventuate among the men.

9 Yous shalt honour thy mates.

Although mateship is not exclusive to the Bogan world, this Digger spirit born in the World War I trenches is a key requirement for participating in the Bogan culture. Loyalty and honesty are incredibly important in the Bogan world. Dobbing in a mate to Centrelink, the police or their other half is the lowest act in the Bogan world.

He's got a pretty alright looking tongue.

10 Be Bogan. Be Proud.

Bogan pride creates incredible self-confidence and fuels a lifelong desire to be taken only as he or she is, and to be judged on character and loyalty not appearance. Once this attitude is embraced, the Bogan is no longer at the mercy of social pressures or fashion, leaving Bogans free to wear clothing that is comfortable and adopt hairstyles that can trigger resentment in certain circles of society.

The UGG

There are great disputes over the origin of the Ugg boot. Some say it was born in the shearing sheds of rural Australia in the 1920s. Others claim it was based on the British World War I flyers' 'fug boots'. Manufacturing mythology claims it was so-named because it was so ugly. Despite the Ugg's disputed origins, what can be agreed on is that the iconic boot took hold in 1970s Australian surf culture, which shared many features of the Bogan world.

But it was not until the 1990s that Ugg boots went global and became a trend alongside AC/DC t-shirts in the big-hair rock scene. Females fast became the primary wearers of the initially unisex Ugg. Bogan females are commonly seen wearing Ugg boots in a great variety of social situations including shopping, karaoke, parties and court appearances.

The BURNOUT

The almost spiritual connection between the Bogan and the automobile cannot be overstated. The Burnout is used to draw attention to and celebrate this association, through the burning of a vehicle's tyres as they spin and create a foul rubber smoke.

The origins of this ritual are unknown, but the popularity of the Burnout in modern Australia can be traced back to 1970s TV shows and movies. Most shows featured a rubber 'peel off': a slight burning of rubber by a muscle car from the era. As the car took off, it would briefly remain stationary, screeching and swerving.

From the 1970s until the late 1990s, the Burnout was considered a harmless but fun use of a vehicle. But with a few serious accidents caused by burnouts going wrong, Bogans were suddenly labelled 'hoons' by tabloid media. From this point, the Burnout evolved into a symbol of fighting authority.

The MULLET

The Mullet is business at the front and a party at the back. Seen in profile, its long, unkempt tail resembles the greasy sea creature after which this unique hairstyle is named.

Although I have traced Mullet-style hair back to the Sphinx in ancient Egypt, it wasn't until the late 1970s and early '80s that the modern Mullet enjoyed its uprising. Iconic Aussies like John Farnham, Warwick Capper and Kylie Minogue helped popularise the style for Bogans, who adopted the look by growing tails on existing haircuts and maintaining their wild Yobbo ways at work.

ORIGINAL MULLET

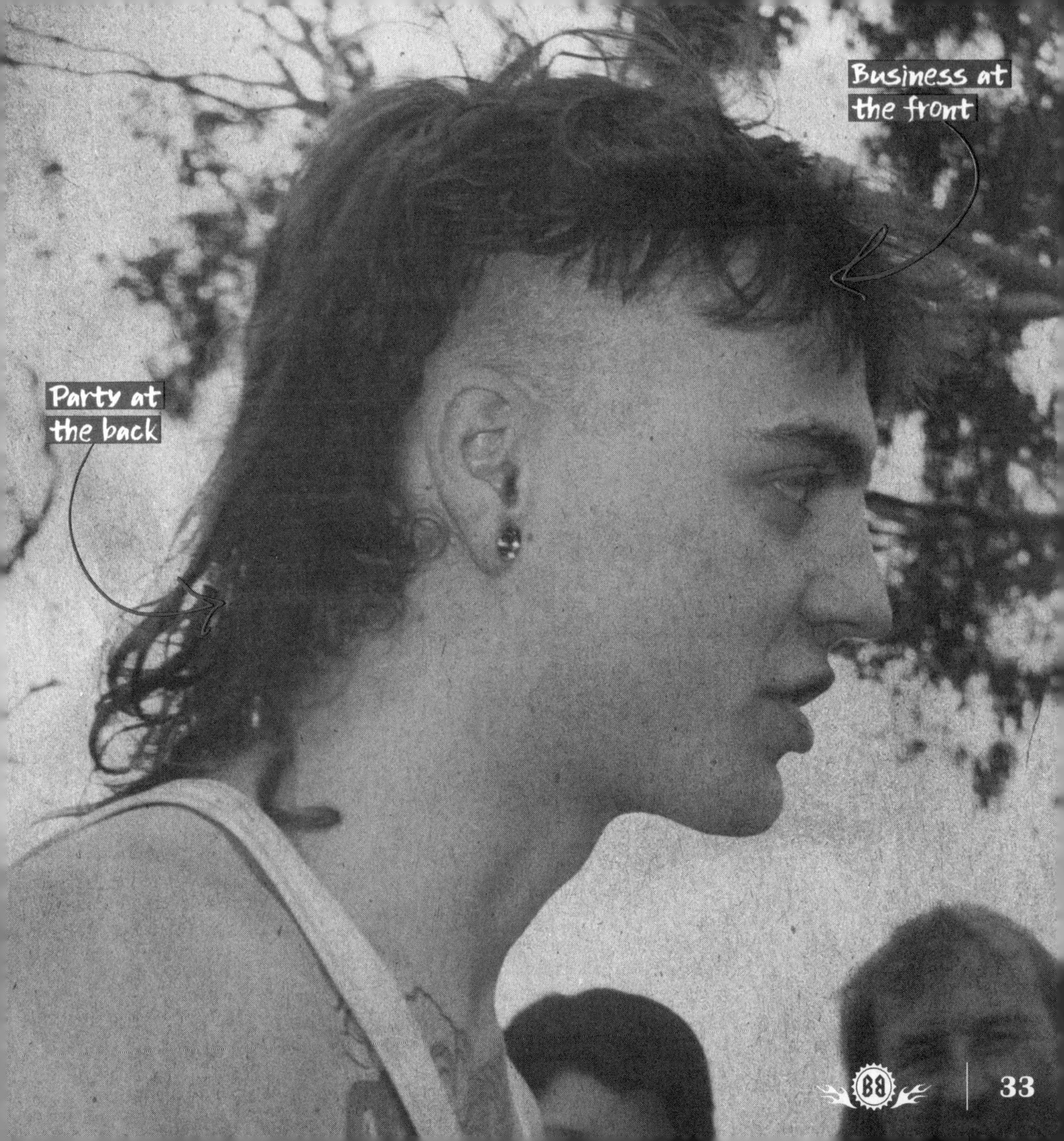

Business at the front

Party at the back

The MULLET

IDENTITY KIT

Classic Mullet

Direct from the pioneering fashionistas of 1984 is the infamous Classic Mullet, an Australian Bogan icon and descendent of hippy rockers and car enthusiasts.

Chick Mullet

This type of Mullet is becoming rare as many younger females now use hair extensions to refashion their appearance. Old-school female Bogans are more of the 'take me like I am or get stuffed' attitude when it comes to both fashion and grooming.

IDENTITY KIT

Skullet

The head is shaved, with one or more long rat-tails remaining. This creates the 'Ratty Mullet'. Bogans who wear this style are often banned from public institutions and places of business as some in authority deem the hairstyle offensive.

Drullet

Often Bogans who smoke excessive amounts of 'weed' endure a strange side effect: their hair gradually becomes dreadlocked and a 'Drullet' begins to form. The metamorphosis takes around three months.

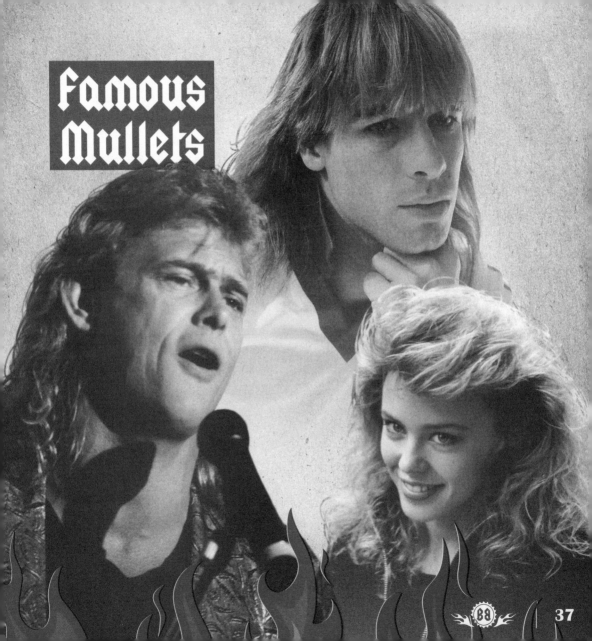

Famous Mullets

LEGENDS

Ned Kelly

The Bogan world has many icons but none are as revered as the original gangster himself, Ned Kelly. Why is Ned so popular in Bogan folklore? The reasons are both historic and cultural.

Many a Bogan can trace their genealogy back to the early convict days. And it is this genetic memory of hating authority that gives rise to the idolising of Australia's greatest bushwhacker. His anti-authoritarian stance is a Bogan ideal – a Bogan Robin Hood, if you like. He fought the unjust corrupt authorities and didn't sell out to mainstream society. He was a true individual. These traits are still valued in Bogans today.

BOGAN
D.I.Y.
SPA and HOT TUB

In the often lower-income world of the Bogan (apart from Cashed-Up Bogans), expensive luxuries are almost non-existent. During summer and winter, this is combatted with a 'fart cart'. Follow the instructions and you can have a completely unique bathing or recreational experience.

Step 1.

Park your ute in the backyard, preferably under the Hills hoist. If you don't own a ute, borrow a mate's – in the Bogan world, four out of five males own some sort of vehicle with a back tray.

Step 2.

Find a large tarpaulin. Again, in this multifaceted flannelette-wearing culture, four out of five males will always have a spare 'tarp'. Place this into the tray of your ute.

Step 3.

Find a length of garden hose that has not been butchered to make bong parts. Attach the hose to a water supply (for hot water, use a tap accessory) and fill the tray of the ute.

step 4.

Attach goon bags and other alcohol, or Bunnings sausages, to the Hills hoist using pegs.

Step 5.

Strip to your underwear, or get naked if your fellow Bogans don't mind seeing 'what you had for breakfast'. You are now at the height of Bogan indulgence. Feel free to make as much noise as possible and splash children, pets and partners that venture within range.

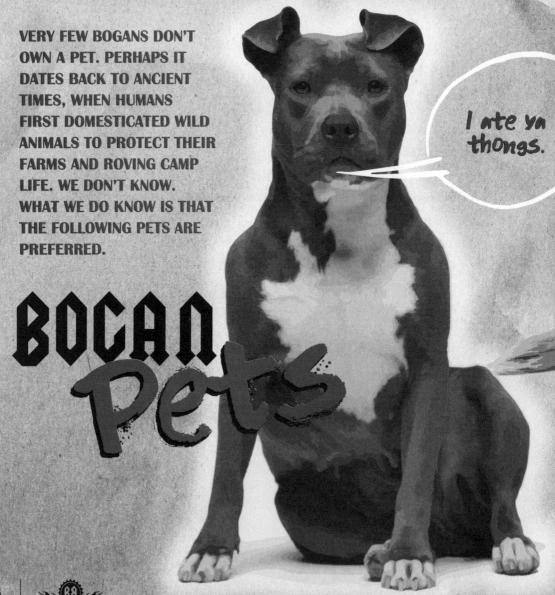

VERY FEW BOGANS DON'T OWN A PET. PERHAPS IT DATES BACK TO ANCIENT TIMES, WHEN HUMANS FIRST DOMESTICATED WILD ANIMALS TO PROTECT THEIR FARMS AND ROVING CAMP LIFE. WE DON'T KNOW. WHAT WE DO KNOW IS THAT THE FOLLOWING PETS ARE PREFERRED.

I ate ya thongs.

BOGAN Pets

I just pissed in ya Uggs.

DOGS

Blue Heelers have an incredible attachment to the Bogan male. Possibly due to the cultural demands of name abbreviation, the 'Bluey' is the most popular pet for a Bogan. Running a close second is the Staffordshire bull terrier or 'Staffy'. This very popular breed of dog charts its popularity back to early TV episodes of *Skippy* where it featured in many scenarios. Another theory is that 'Staffy' sounds like 'stiffy' and this phallic confusion contributes to the breed's popularity.

BOGAN Pets

Bite Me!

FERRETS

This angry, smelly, noisy little creature appeals to many males and females in the culture. Perhaps it's the similarities shared with the Bogan owner?

FICHTING FISH

Sales of these sea creatures in Bogan areas are the highest of all water-dwelling pets. Sadly, many Bogans expect a much more violent outcome and the fish become neglected: 'I thought the slimy buggers'd get it on like UFC? They just swim around doin' sweet FA.'

BOGAN Pets

> If Rolf tries to tie me down I'll go him.

KANGAROOS

In rare cases, Bogans in remote areas raise kangaroos as pets. Although this practice is illegal, many ignore the law and share a close bond with this truly Australian piece of fauna.

SNAKES ►

Very popular with Boganite teenagers and Bogans who ride motorcycles. Snake ownership oftens leads to a sub-pet ownership: mice (food for the snake).

◄ LIZARDS

In Bogan subcultures the uglier the pet, the greater the interest. Lizards are extremely popular for this reason.

Belly
of the Bogans

IDENTIFYING BOGANS BY ABDOMINAL VERIFICATION

NOT SURE IF YOU ARE IN THE COMPANY OF A BOGAN? A SIMPLE SCAN OF THE STOMACH AREA CAN PROVIDE CONFIRMATION.

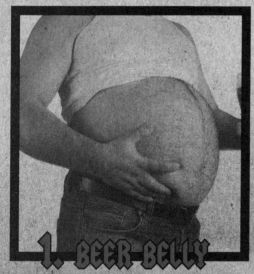

1. BEER BELLY

Years of work go into a gut like this. Hours spent at pubs, BBQs and watching sport on TV create the billowing belly.

2. TOO MANY TATTS CUT

Self-explanatory. The stomach region has an incredible array of poorly done or silly tattoos.

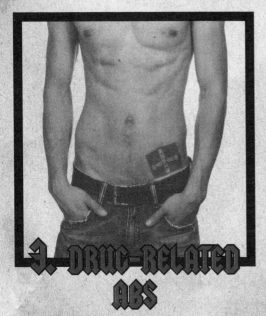

3. DRUG-RELATED ABS

This mid-section is found on Bogans who partake in too many illegal drugs. It does prove though that if you want to lose weight, there are options besides Jenny Craig.

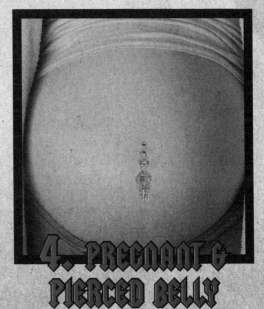

4. PREGNANT & PIERCED BELLY

Found on the younger female Bogan. It often comes with a stretched-out tattoo depicting the Southern Cross.

BOGAN Movies

A SIX-PACK OF BOGAN MOVIES

Kenny

Only a Bogan would fall in love with a movie about portaloos.

▷

Crocodile Dundee

Still a favourite among Bogans, the hobby bushman attitude is familiar to the modern Bogan.

▽

△

Muriel's Wedding

A Bogan spin on the Ugly Duckling classic. With ABBA.

Housos vs Authority

Just a bloody great movie.

Wake in Fright

Bogans getting pissed and causing mayhem in the outback.

The Adventures of Barry McKenzie

A precursor to modern Boganism, this film predicted the drinking, the hate for authority, the mateship. A film ahead of its time.

LEGENDS

Kath & Kim

Although some Bogans feel they are a piss-take of a proud species, Kath & Kim are widely considered the high priestesses of Lady Boganhood. Loud, proud and effluent in the manner of many Cashed-Up Bogans, their mother–daughter fashions (Uggs, trackies, thongs and bum-floss G-strings) and love of a chat while drinking 'cardonnay' (casked), Cruisers (bottled), Cosmopolitans (jugged) or vodka (jellied) have made their catchphrases a staple at many Australian BBQs.

BOGAN BABY Names

STUDIES SHOW THAT BOGANS LIKE TO BE INVENTIVE AND UNIQUE WHEN IT COMES TO NAMING THEIR OFFSPRING

Daxon

Izaak

J'zayden

Zabryn

Khodii

Macsen

Dazza

Jathon

Brogan

Blade

WHEN YOU CAN'T PICK BETWEEN TWO NAMES, DON'T! COMBINE THEM INTO ONE:

Zack + Tyler = Zyler

Jarrod + Darren = Jarren

Cheryldine

Beautiful

Braelyn

Shazza

Kyly

D'ynell

Ever

Kazza

WHEN TRYING TO COME UP WITH SOMETHING UNUSUAL, WHY NOT TAKE A COMMON WORD AND REVERSE IT?

Heaven becomes Neveah

Divine becomes Enivid

Truly

Younique

McKyla

The 40-YEAR-OLD NANNA

In the '70s and '80s, many Bogans were having children very young. As the years went on, their children also bred young. Thus we have a common Bogan sight: The 40-year-old Nanna. She generally has about four children. These children each usually have another three or four children themselves. The 40-year-old Nan often does much of the childrearing. She becomes the matriarch of the family and the centre of the world for both her children and her grandchildren. The Nanna is, in almost every instance, fiercely patriotic to Australia. When money is scarce, the 40-year-old Nanna will always help her offspring. She has a heart of gold and, despite much adversity in life, strives and thrives in the harsh outer Bogan lands of Australia.

BOGAN D.I.Y. FLOAT TANK

In times of dire need, to cool off in the harsh Australian summer and sometimes just to wash away the hangover Bogans will use the common council recycle bin as a bath or personal float tank*. To adjust the original design, wrap the base in alfoil and put a fire underneath. This will warm the bin, creating a jacuzzi effect.

* Not to be used by anyone under the height of the bin itself.

Darren Williams

Darren Williams from Tasmania was crowned Australia's Greatest Bogan during the TV series called *Bogan Hunters*. He carries a personal attitude of generosity and, as you can see by his photo, he displays many great Bogan qualities. He isn't influenced by fashion. He has a minor Mullet but it is well cared for. He loves motorsports. In fact, Darren loves motorsports a little too much. Incredibly, he has over 75 minor driving offences, ranging from driving unlicensed to burnout offences across the Apple Isle. A judge once described him as 'the second worst driver in Tasmania'. This second-place accolade is further proof of his great Boganicity. Being the worst driver would be overachieving.

Bogans at work

IT IS A COMMON MISCONCEPTION THAT BOGANS ARE 'BLUDGERS'.
IN FACT, BOGANS FORM A LARGE PART OF THE AUSTRALIAN ECONOMY
AND THEIR WORKPLACES ARE NUMEROUS AND VARIED.

THE TRADIE

Identifiable by the short shorts, blue singlet and Blundstone
boots, Tradie Bogans can fix anything and everything.
There's no job too small for them to not overcharge you.
You'll know their nose is to the grindstone when they
honour you with the 'brickie's smile' or 'plumber's crack'.

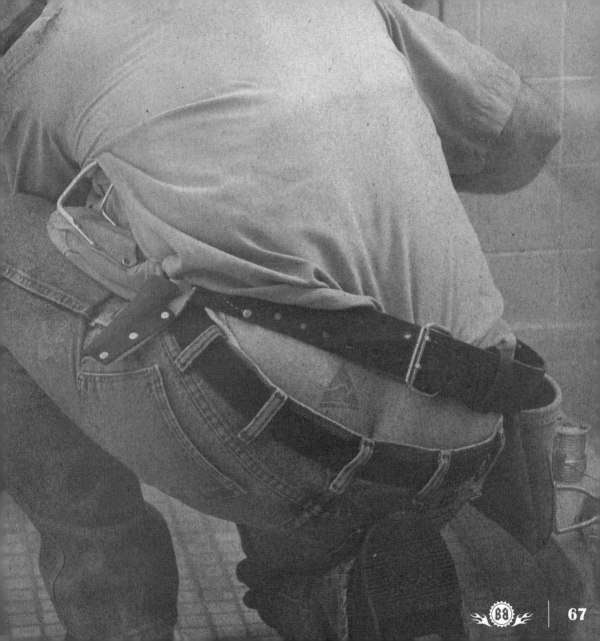

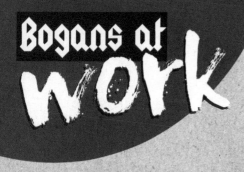

Bogans at work

TRANSPORT

Bogans keep our country moving and occupy key positions in traffic control across the country. Often they are texting other Bogans while operating the Stop and Go signs at primary schools. More likely they will be sitting in, or leaning on, one of the various 'support' vehicles at construction sites, looking at free porn on their outdated mobile phones.

Pie 'n' beer? Snitty 'n' beer? Parma 'n' beer? So many choices . . .
TRAFFIC CONTROL

Bogans at work

SPORT

Bogans can be found in many of the nation's Aussie Rules, rugby league, cricket, shooting and dwarf-throwing teams. Bristling moustaches, hairy legs and multiple tattoos abound in both male and female sporting squads, making this unique breed of Bogan revered in public and very well paid.

Unlike their less famous Bogan cousins, these sportspeople are able to procreate with a better quality of Bogan and even, occasionally, non-Bogans.

Bogans at work

MINING

This modern breed of Aussie Digger spends long periods underground or offshore. Mining booms across our land have resulted in Bogan workers with basic trades and skills earning double and triple your average Bogan wage.

Bogans at work

POLITICS

Bogans are natural born leaders and specialise in 'keeping the bastards honest'. Former beer-sculling champion Bob Hawke became prime minister after the Bogan boom of the late '70s. And when Australia's first female Bogan PM, Julia Gillard, handed over the keys to her brown brick home in Altona in 2015, she left a traditional Bogan housewarming gift for the new owners: her Ugg boots.

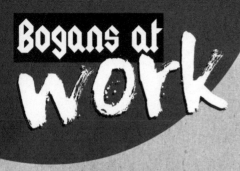

Bogans at work

CASHED-UP BOGAN

Cashed-Up Bogans can be identified by their glowing white teeth created in cheap dental surgeries in Thailand. In the case of the female Bogan, a breast enlargement is sometimes completed at the same time. For male Bogans a sleeve tattoo often accessorises the new teeth.

The SICKIE

The Sickie was part of Bogan work culture until John Howard brought in WorkChoices and subsequent other schemes designed to make the Australian population more productive. In the past, the Sickie was a frowned upon but accepted practice, but under WorkChoices it became a sackable offence. The Sickie – once a source of joy to the Bogan – went the way of the Dodo.

Foolproof Bogan Sickie excuses:

'I think I've come down with a 24-hour tumour.'

'I gobbled the wrong goon and now I'm cacking in my trackies.'

BOGAN Landmarks

Bogans go big or go home. And when they're not home, they're on the road going big with things like pineapples, bananas, prawns, merino sheep ... and Bogans!

NO. 1 BOGAN ERECTION

AS VOTED BY ALL BOGANS

The crème de la crème of these massive structures is in the town of Nyngan. In the Bogan Shire, on the banks of the Bogan River, there is an actual Big Bogan. A five-metre-tall statue of a Bogan complete with mullet, thongs, esky, singlet and fishing rod. An incredible tribute to the NSW inland bogan.

BOGAN TOWN PLANNING

STUDIES SHOW THAT BOGANS PREFER TO LIVE IN TOWNS LIKE THE ONE SHOWN HERE.

CENO AND COP SHOP

The Centrelink office, or 'Ceno', is always within 5 degrees of city centre. A cop shop is the Bogan's best friend and there is always one nearby.

PETROL STATION AND 7/11

Two petrol stations with 7/11 refreshments and kebab stand on site or nearby.

SWIMMING POOL

A place where grommets can cause trouble.

CLUBS AND PUBS

Out of the centre, there are at least two or three large pubs and clubs set within the major concentration of suburbia.

FAST FOODCHAINS

A plethora of fast food restaurants, the most popular being Maccas and KFC. Due to the low incomes of Bogans, these food choices are generally economic.

SHOPPING CENTRE

A major shopping centre is generally within walking distance.

SCHOOL

A public school for Boganite offspring.

FOOTY OVAL AND PARKLANDS

Parks for nocturnal mischief by teenage Bogans.

HOUSOS

Boganville village always near major parkland and ovals.

Welcome to BOGANVILLE

The VB
(Very Bogan)
XMAS
TREE

This incredible piece of 'Strayan Christmas cheer
was constructed by epic Bogan Wes Boyd (Even Wes's
numberplate reads 'MAD BOGAN').
This is an example of Bogan recycling at its best – 2500 cans
were used in the colossal tribute to the silly season.
Best of all, Wes personally 'sank all the piss' – a feat
that took him just 16 days and established him as one of
the true gold-class Bogans in Western Australia.

How to host a
BOGAN
BBQ

Step 1.

Steal a trolley from your local shopping centre carpark.

Step 2.

Flip the trolley on its side and add wood, old magazines, parking fines and warrants for arrest.

Step 3.

Using petrol, turps, firelighters and/or lighter fluid, soak your wood etc. completely. Light the fuel.

Step 4.

Add sausages and other meat. Under no circumstances should you BBQ fish or any food associated with vegetarianism. As the meat cooks, season your Bogan delicacies with at least three litres of beer.

Step 5.

Once your meat is Dunlop-radial black, place the food in any kind of bread available: hot dog buns, toast bread or French bread if you want to impress a Bogan of the opposite gender.

BOGAN RED SANGRIA RECIPE

If you are having any kind of upmarket Bogan get-together – say a Coon 'n' Goon night (known in non-Bogan circles as a Cheese and Wine Appreciation Evening) – this 'cocktail' is a real summer favourite. Originally a recipe from Spain, it was imported back to Australia by Bogans who participated in the running of the bulls in the early '80s with one key variation – instead of wine, Aussie goon is a must.

INGREDIENTS

1   space bag of fine Aussie red goon
1   large bottle of generic brand cola
1   bag of ice from the service station
1   orange
10 plastic cups

RECIPE

1. Pour three-quarters of the cola into another container. Or the kids.
2. Fill the cola bottle with goon wine.
3. Shove slices of orange through the top of the bottle.
4. Crush ice with a hammer and shove the ice into the bottle.
5. Replace the cap on the bottle and shake. Refrigerate for 3 mins.
6. Take Bogan Sangria from fridge and pour into the plastic cups.
7. Enjoy!

• For White Bogan Sangria, replace red goon with white goon, and cola with lemonade.

Note: White Bogan Sangria is not as popular as the red blend. It can generally be found at the beginning of a Hen's Night just before a taxi is called for the Hens to depart in search of a male strip club.

ORIGIN OF THE BOGAN SPECIES

BOGAN

BIG BANG

The Bogan Big Bang has nothing to do with the origins of time and space or the earliest beginnings of the universe. It's the noise of a Holden Monaro's exhaust pipes as it hoons around industrial areas, or of its engine exploding after too much celebratory backfiring. According to NASA, in the first second after the universe began, the temperature was about 10 billion degrees Fahrenheit – roughly equivalent to the combined heat from the tyres if every Bogan in Australia performed a burnout at the same time.

BOGAN

BC

Cavemen held many similarities to the contemporary Bogan. They lived to party and procreate, and they gathered around fires to cook the flesh of beasts while telling bullshit stories. Then as now, clothing was minimal. Skins and pelts were worn with pride, as Bogans wear Uggs and leather jackets today. Wild facial hair and crude tattoos were worn to show virility (pre-Viagra). Ultimately this led to BC Bogans of Egypt building the Sphinx, a creature half-man (i.e. Bogan) and half-lion (i.e. a Holden-owner), which wore a mullet hairstyle – proving without doubt that man's Bogan tendencies are ancient indeed.

Prehistoric Mullet

Early Cricket bat

Neolithic goatee

Early Mag Wheel

Early thongs and Uggs made from brontosaurus foreskins.

BOGAN

MESSIAH

There are too many mythological similarities between the Bogan and the Messiah to ignore. Both were thongs, Jesus preferring the leather variety. Both sport a beard and long hair, Jesus wearing his in a 'Nazareth Mullet'. Jesus was a carpenter by trade and would have been handy under the bonnet of a GTX Falcon. The story of Jesus making goon from water describes an early form of Bogan homebrew – and a trick often attempted by modern Bogans when the bottle shop down the road is closed.

BOGAN

FIRST FLEET

These days, getting pissed on a cruise ship is considered a great Bogan holiday. But Bogan scholars have charted its popularity back to Captain Cook's epic voyage of discovery from England to the Great Southern Land in 1770. Cook's diary has many references to his crew wearing flannelette to keep warm, drinking way too much grog and overeating pies and charred meats during the voyage. By the time Arthur Phillip led the First Fleet to Botany Bay – also known as Bogany Bay – with a shipload of convicts in 1788, the Bogan spirit had truly found its spiritual home.

BOGAN
UPRISINGS

Bogans are anti-authoritarian and their rebel roots are many. The first great rebellion in Australia's history was the 1808 Rum Rebellion. But the first truly Bogan uprising was the Eureka Stockade in 1854. Conventional historians say that this great Aussie rebellion was about miners demanding rights, but recent archeological discoveries have found it was not much more than a giant piss-up Bogan-style. Basically, a bunch of miners with Bogan tendencies got very drunk and decided that they hated the local authority. And, like all Bogans, their priorities were clear: cheaper alcohol and tobacco.

BOGAN

BABY BOOMERS

Modern Aussie Boganism begins in the mid-70s. It was a cross-breeding of several species of Australian humanity: convict rebels, factory girls and Digger kids.

One of the bastard children of this Bogan gene splicing was the Yobbo. Yobbos loved watching cricket in summer and footy in winter. Spotting a Yobbo was easy. Males usually wore t-shirts with slogans like 'Free moustache rides' while females wore denim cut-offs and – in keeping with the more liberated times – went bra-less. Compulsory footwear for men and women of this era was rubber thongs, worn in all weather conditions.

BOGANS 2.0
MODERN

Whether filthy rich or dirt poor, modern Bogans are easy to spot. Modern Gentleman Bogans (MGBs) are still most commonly found near BBQs, garages and man-sheds foraging for TV sport, beer, jet-ski manuals, beer … or crime and sports books, while listening to Cold Chisel, The Twelfth Man or Powderfinger. Modern Lady Bogans (MLBs) meanwhile are loud, proud and liberated and will gather in large flocks to watch reality TV, listen to Kylie Minogue, and drink pre-mix cocktails.

BOGANS 3.0

FUTURE

Although the Bogan population is strong, political correctness threatens their very survival. Over-regulation of work places and social meeting spots, coupled with general media discrimination, make the Bogan's future uncertain. Will this most gregarious of Australian DNA strands crack under the pressure of authorities hell-bent on eradicating them? Or does the future see the Aussie Pride gene explode to all four corners of the earth with Bogans becoming the dominant species on the planet?

The THONG

That classic Bogan footwear, the Aussie Thong actually originated in ancient Egypt. Although in modern times the footwear is constructed with rubber, back then they were made using goat testicles and leather strips from a pig's buttocks. Throughout history, many different cultures have adopted this design but none with the passion or enthusiasm of the Aussie Bogan.

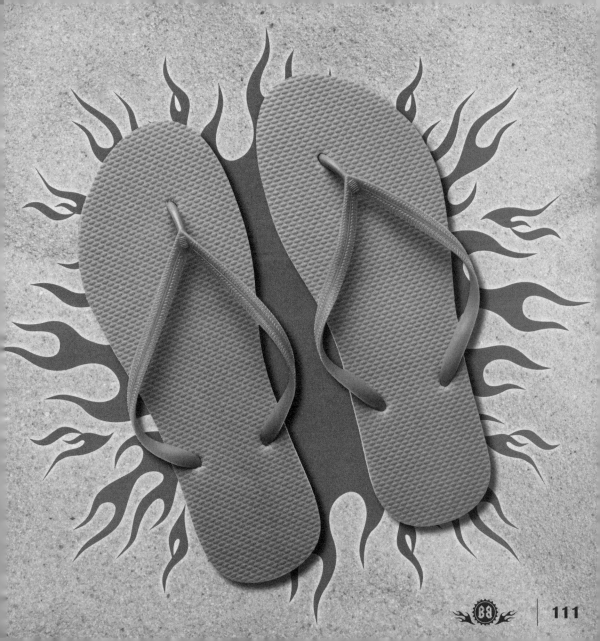

The THONG

FACTS

1

Early Thong-innovators employed various materials, ranging from wood to seaweed, to woven grass, cheap plastic and modern rubber.

2

The Thong's introduction to the modern Western world was after World War II. Soldiers returning home from the war in Japan brought home pairs of *zori*, a flexible battle sandal made from cherry blossoms, bamboo and seaweed and made famous by samurai warriors and kamikaze pilots.

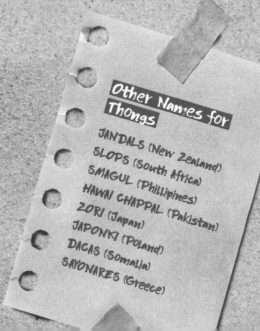

Other Names for Thongs

JANDALS (New Zealand)
SLOPS (South Africa)
SMAGUL (Phillipines)
HAWAI CHAPPAL (Pakistan)
ZORI (Japan)
JAPONKI (Poland)
DACAS (Somalia)
SAYONARES (Greece)

3

From here, American companies cashed in on this ancient design, creating rubber thongs. The USA changed the name of the Thong to 'flip-flop' after the sound it made while being walked in.

5

In the 1980s, Americans changed the name of a G-string (an undergarment covering the genitals) to a 'thong'. This led to much confusion with Aussie Bogans travelling to the USA and in need of footwear. Many Bogans seeking thongs found themselves in lingerie shops, completely confused.

4

The mass-produced version of the Thong was introduced to Australia in 1959 by the Dunlop company (although the Brazilians released a version of the Thong called Havaianas in the 1960s). The Aussie Bogan quickly saw how perfect this form of footwear was for the hot Australian summer.

The THONG ANATOMY

✓ **Zero effort** (very appealing to Bogans)

✓ **No laces**

✓ **No chance of foot odour due to open-air design**

✓ **Waterproof**

✓ **Resistant to hot sand and bitumen roads**

✓ **Able to be worn to both worksites and weddings**

INTERESTING USES OF THE THONG

1. SPRAY MASK

2. THONG G-STRING

3. WEAPON OF CHOICE

In 1973, a legendary band led by two brothers, Angus and Malcolm Young, was born. With Scottish-born Aussie singer Bon Scott, AC/DC developed a sound and attitude that would sink deep into the souls of Bogans all over the country. AC/DC – or Acca Dacca as fans came to know them – played coast-to-coast, on trucks, on roofs and in Australia's roughest pubs. Fights broke out. Beer was guzzled by the metric tonne. Homemade tattoos were born. And many teeth were lost either by a punch to the face or too many bourbon and Cokes. After AC/DC gigs, spirits were high among male and female Bogans. Car parks, couches and Holden back-seats became breeding grounds and modern Bogan Aussie pride was born.

The B'DAY PIE

A gastronomical creation unique to Bogan culture is the Birthday Pie. Seen at celebrations around Australia, this gourmet treat is a simple construction of service-station pies and candles. Generally, there are multiple Birthday Pies arranged in a pyramid for the party as one alone would not meet the needs of partygoers. If attempting to create your own pie cake, make sure you reheat the pie at home in a microwave, never use an oven. This will guarantee the classic soggy pie effect cherished in the Bogan world.

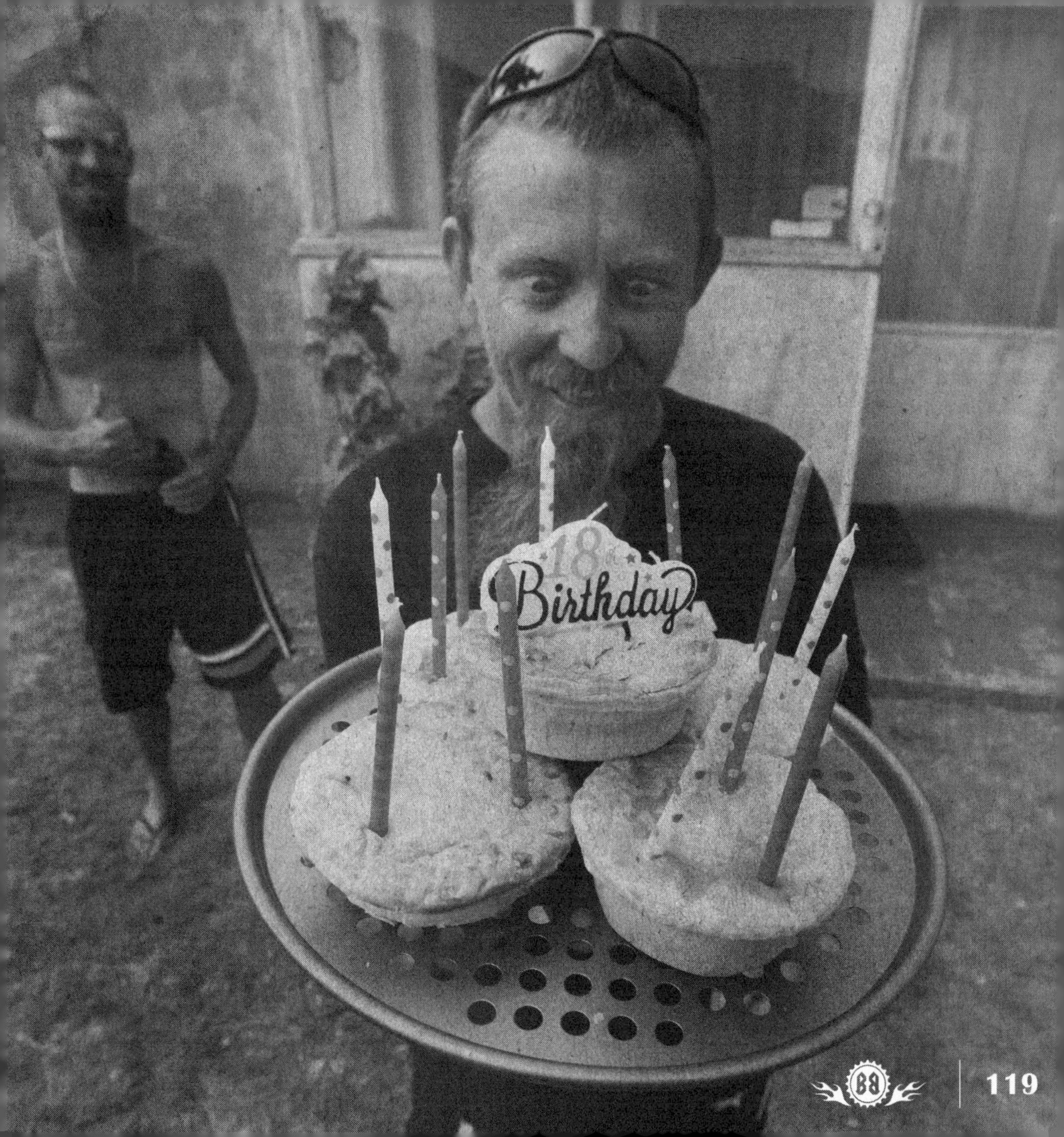
18th
Birthday

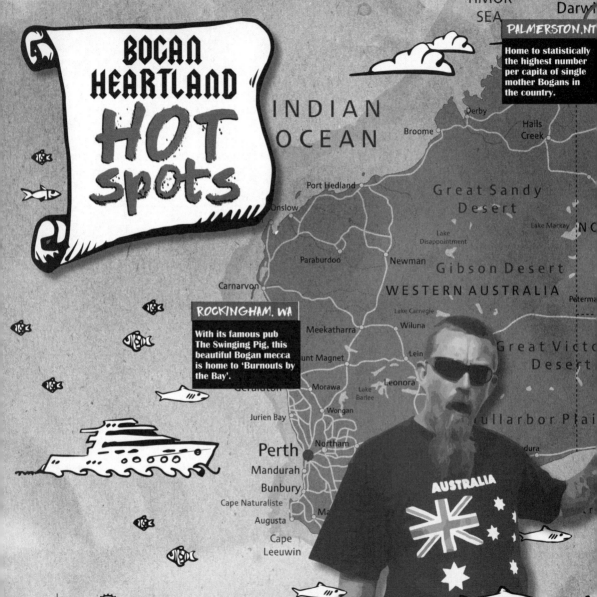

BOGAN HEARTLAND HOT spots

Darwi

INDIAN OCEAN

PALMERSTON, NT
Home to statistically the highest number per capita of single mother Bogans in the country.

ROCKINGHAM, WA
With its famous pub The Swinging Pig, this beautiful Bogan mecca is home to 'Burnouts by the Bay'.

Derby
Broome
Halls Creek

Port Hedland
Onslow

Great Sandy Desert
Lake Mackay
N

Lake Disappointment

Paraburdoo
Newman
Gibson Desert

Carnarvon
WESTERN AUSTRALIA

Peterma

Lake Carnegie
Meekatharra
Wiluna
Great Victo
Deser

unt Magnet
Lein

Geraldton
Morawa
Leonora

Lake Barlee
Wongan
ullarbor Plai

Jurien Bay

Perth
Northam

Mandurah
AUSTRALIA

Bunbury

Cape Naturaliste
Ma

Augusta

Cape Leeuwin

ROCKHAMPTON. QLD

'Bogans by the beach' is a way this suburb is sometimes described. An incredible treasure trove of burnouts, beers and bongs. It is believed to have the highest concentration of Bogans in a coastal city.

LOGAN. QLD

Logan is home to the infamous Logan Bogan. Mullets, ciggies, thongs and home-done tattoos make this a Queensland Bogan extravaganza.

BUDGEWOI. NSW

Incredible Bogan town with a younger population of 'lads', 'housos' and garden-variety Boganisms. Interestingly, you cannot gain employment in many businesses in this town if you don't have at least four tattoos.

ELIZABETH. SA

A top-shelf hive of black label Bogans.

FRANKSTON. VIC

Although it has recently attempted to shake off its Bogan image, the city has more tattoo shops than any other city in the country. Frankston's most popular baby names are Sharon, Darren and Kylie.

CANBERRA. ACT

In recent years, with more and more Bogan political figures in our capital (Pauline Hanson, Jacqui Lambie, Bob Katter) the parliament, although not a suburb, is the most Bogan place in this territory.

Marrawah

Strathgordon

Hoba

The southern-most point of Australia is home to the purest breed of Bogan nature has to offer. Typically either rail thin or 'obeasty' (a delightful if crude fusion of 'obese' and 'beasty'), the Tassie Bogan consumes almost no vegetables and subsists on steak, sausages, bread and milk. When travelling to Tasmania, you can't miss these beautiful blue-blood Bogans in their natural habitat. Recent studies have shown that, due to the island's isolation and the interbreeding of Bogan relatives, a rare Bogan gene has appeared in Tasmanian DNA. It's called *Boganus Tasmanius*. The gene makes the person more likely to 'hot up' a car, listen to AC/DC and generally rebel against authority.

BOGAN
D.I.Y.
OUTDOOR LOUNGE

For Bogans who are handy, this outdoor lounge is as easy as a trip to the supermarket carpark and borrowing a welder. Not recommended in the high temperatures of summer.

NORM

In the 1970s the first animated Bogan character appeared on our TV screens. In an effort to encourage the Australian population to be more physically active, the government created Norm. Norm was the star of the 'Life. Be in it' series of TV commercials and print advertisements. He was a fat guy who lounged around, usually watching TV.

This was the first government attempt at attacking Bogan culture. Thankfully the spirit of Norm prevailed. Bogans did occasionally get out of the house and ignore the Test match on TV but by and large they raised a defiant finger. Why should they be in it? To be told what to do, even by a cartoon, was an attack on their personal freedoms.

BOGAN APPROVED LANGUAGE

Spoken across many towns and suburbs of Australia is a dialect I like to call 'Boganese'. This language, like all colourful derivatives, has certain sounds and patterns.

Many Bogans run words together and show little or no lip movement. For example, a simple sentence such as 'Hi, how are you today?' becomes 'Heyhowyagoinmaate'.

The female Bogan generally speaks at a much higher volume and pitch, and will accent most sentences with a derogatory comment, approval-seeking or heartfelt empathy for a fellow Bogan who has been wronged.

SPORT

Cricket, rugby league, AFL, motorsports, boxing and mixed martial arts i.e. cage fighting are all welcome. Do not mention soccer: it is a sport to be derided. Be aware, team rivalries may lead to conversations that end with police intervention.

Mate, you're thick in the head! Anyone who thinks Collingwood isn't gonna win is mad!

VEHICLES

Top-shelf Bogans will own either a Holden or Ford. Much of the day is passed discussing their own vehicles, or vehicles spotted in their day-to-day life. Vehicle specifics are often shared ('She's a V8 with a drinks holder on the tow bar. How good is that?') as are comparisons to others ('Your car's a bomb made in China') as well as any merchandising associated with vehicles.

Want a cuppa in me Peter Brock memorial mug?

FASHION

Hair and makeup are not priorities in the Bogan world, but without the distinct Bogan fashion, many of the species would be unable to recognise their fellow Bogans.

RELIGION

I got nuffin against Buddha. I got a tattoo of him from me trip to Bali. It's next to me tattoo of the kids' names and birthdays... so I remember 'em.

POLITICS

**This is fine to discuss because a Bogan's knowledge
of the subject is limited.**

Which one's
the prime
minister again?
The fat one,
the wanker or
Pauline Hanson?

TRANSLATIONS

If engaging in conversation with someone of the Bogan species, use some of the following sentences to make the Bogan feel comfortable in your presence.

'Howyagarn?'
'Hello. Pleased to meet you.'

'Yourshout.'
'I believe it's customary for you to buy the next drink.'

'Mateyousgoalright.'
'I think highly of you, friend.'

'Pullyaheadin.'
'I think you're behaving inappropriately.'

LOOSER TRANSLATIONS

'Getadogupyers.'

There is much conjecture as to the meaning of this sentence. However, if said in a pub, generally speaking it is an invitation to purchase and consume an alcoholic beverage.

'Tits or rubber – one or the other!'

This expression is commonly heard at car enthusiast events. When Bogan couples drive their hot cars around the venue, it is customary for crowds to demand 'rubber' (a burnout) or 'tits' (encouraging the female to bear her upper half). Similar expressions are found at Bogan schoolies events: male Boganites will shout **'Titsoutfortheboys!'** *to which the female Boganites will issue the rallying cry* **'Dicksoutforthechicks!'**

GREAT BOGAN INVENTIONS

Rideable Esky

In the Bogan world there can be many situations where beer must be transported ASAP. The rideable esky is the premier delivery service. It was invented in 1973 by a farmer in Ballarat who did not own a car. Rather than carry an esky three kilometres to his mate's property and risk a warm tinny, he constructed a makeshift esky-wagon to transport himself and some beers into Bogan infamy.

The THONG TAG

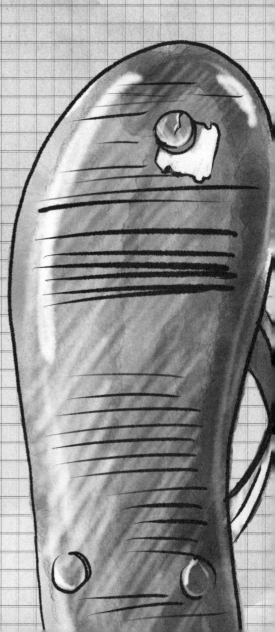

Thongs are as hard-wearing and tough as their Bogan owners. But sometimes they come unplugged. This can be dangerous if a Bogan has to walk across hot sand, driveway cement hotter than the sun or road bitumen bubbling on a summer's day. The answer, pioneered (but never patented) by Bogans, is to push the plug through the hole and snap on one of those clips found on plastic bread bags.

1. Bogan Un-plugged? Not an acoustic album but a thong gone bung.

2. Simply poke the doolacky back through the busted hole.

3. Grab a tag from a bread bag and clip on. Good for at least 72 hours (or five bottlo visits).

The UTE

Not invented by Holden in Adelaide but Ford in Geelong, this brilliant Bogan chariot is basically a mullet on wheels with a sedan cabin up front and a small truck out back. The brainwave of Bogan engineer Lewis Bandt in 1934, it has become a favourite of tradies, farmers and horny al fresco Bogans who consider no Ute Muster complete without a 'lay in the tray' (then a post-orgasm burnout).

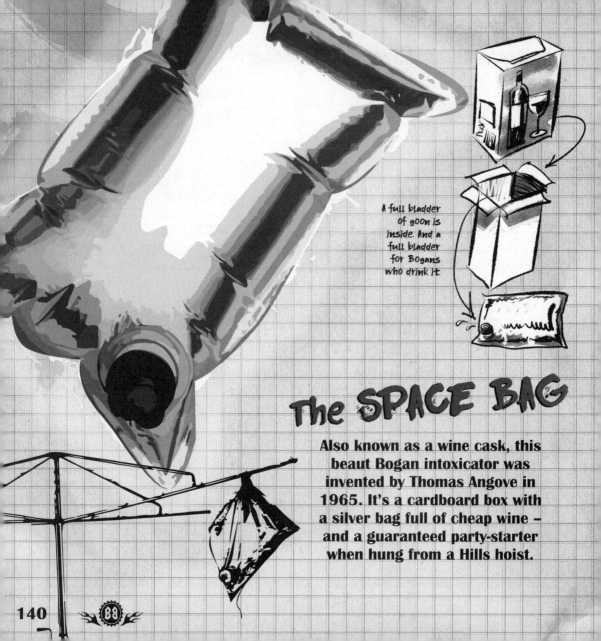

A full bladder of goon is inside. And a full bladder for Bogans who drink it.

The SPACE BAG

Also known as a wine cask, this beaut Bogan intoxicator was invented by Thomas Angove in 1965. It's a cardboard box with a silver bag full of cheap wine – and a guaranteed party-starter when hung from a Hills hoist.

DIM SIMS and CHIKO ROLLS

Bogan cuisine is famous throughout the world. Its two greatest gifts to the gourmet planet are the Dim Sim – invented by Melbourne's William Wing Young in 1945 – and the Chiko Roll, which Frank McEncroe invented by putting a batter on chop suey (aka Bogan leftovers), frying it then serving it at the Wagga Wagga show in 1951.

55·8 mtr

3·93°

84·7°

60°

Pissed Bogans often 'lean' into a Chiko Roll at 3am on the same angle as the Tower of Pisa.

13·5cm

GRAB A CHIKO

20°

INTO A CHIKO

CHIKO

GET INTO A CHIKO

CHIKO

GET INTO A CHIKO

CHIKO

GET INTO A CHIKO

CHIKO

GET INTO A CHIKO

BEER GOGGLES

The invention of 'beer goggles' is essential to the continuation of the Bogan tribe. During the mating ritual of most Bogans, alcohol (or other substances) is paramount.

1. It begins when a Bogan scans the room and recognises a Bogan of the opposite sex. At this point, the beer goggles remain in the 'off' position.

2. After several beverages the Bogan beer goggles are switched to 'standby'.
(Can I buy you a drink?)

3. After a skinful, a Bogan's beer goggles are fully activated and courtship can commence.
(Hey baby, want an Aussie kiss? It's like a French one but down under)

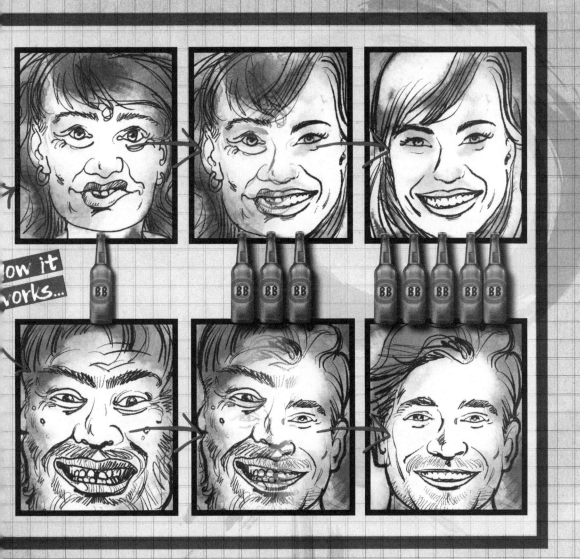

BOGAN D.I.Y. PORTALOO

In the Bogan world, the call of nature can appear without warning. The male Bogan has no difficulty urinating in public places at any time, and after dark the same can be said of the female Bogan. But what do you do if it's not just a simple pee-pee? Grab a traffic cone and go for gold!

ARE YOU A BOGAN ?

MANY AUSTRALIANS HAVE THE BOGAN WITHIN THEM. SOME ALREADY CELEBRATE THIS, OTHERS SADLY DENY IT. CHALLENGE YOUR MUM, DAD, SISTER, BROTHER, COUSIN AND YOURSELF TO THIS TEST TO FIND OUT IF YOU'VE BEEN TOUCHED BY THE GRACE OF BOGAN CULTURE.

1. **HAVE YOU EVER HAD A MULLET HAIRCUT?**

   Yes ☐ No ☐

2. **HAVE YOU BEEN TO THE BATHURST 1000?**

   Yes ☐ No ☐

3. **DO YOU WATCH THE BATHURST 1000?**

   Yes ☐ No ☐

4. **DO YOU ENJOY AC/DC, BARNESY OR ANY OTHER AUSSIE '70S OR '80S ROCK AND ROLL MUSICIANS?**

   Yes ☐ No ☐

5. **DO YOU HAVE MORE THAN THREE TATTOOS?**

   Yes ☐ No ☐

6. **HAVE YOU TAKEN A SICK DAY TO WATCH A SPORTING EVENT ON TV?**

   Yes ☐ No ☐

7. **IF YOU MOWED YOUR FRONT LAWN, WOULD YOU FIND VEHICLES YOU FORGOT YOU OWN?**

   Yes ☐ No ☐

8. **HAVE YOU EVER HAD SEX IN THE BACK SEAT OF A HOLDEN, FORD, TRAIN OR BUS?**

   Yes ☐ No ☐

9. **DO YOU HAVE LONG DISCUSSIONS WITH MATES ABOUT RUGBY LEAGUE, AFL OR CRICKET?**

☐ Yes ☐ No

10. **DO YOU WEAR THONGS IN SUMMER?**

☐ Yes ☐ No

11. **HAVE YOU EVER MODIFIED A VEHICLE?**

☐ Yes ☐ No

12. **DO YOU WEAR UGGS IN WINTER?**

☐ Yes ☐ No

13. **HAVE YOU AVOIDED VISITING A DENTIST FOR MORE THAN THREE YEARS?**

☐ Yes ☐ No

14. **DOES YOUR THREE-MONTH-OLD AND YOUR DE FACTO HAVE THE SAME AMOUNT OF TEETH?**

☐ Yes ☐ No

15. **DO YOU DRINK MORE THAN TWO CANS OF BEER A DAY, ON AVERAGE?**

☐ Yes ☐ No

16. **HAVE YOU EVER PLAYED 'GOBBLE THE GOON'?**

☐ Yes ☐ No

17. **DO YOU KNOW HOW TO CONSTRUCT A HOME-MADE BONG?**

☐ Yes ☐ No

18. DO ANY OF YOUR RELATIVES RESIDE IN A CARAVAN?

☐ Yes ☐ No

19. HAVE YOU EVER DONE A BURNOUT?

☐ Yes ☐ No

20. DO ANY OF YOUR CHILDREN HAVE TATTOOS?

☐ Yes ☐ No

21. DO YOU USE AN ESKY MORE THAN THREE TIMES A YEAR?

☐ Yes ☐ No

22. HAVE YOU EVER SCULLED MORE THAN FOUR BEERS IN ONE SITTING?

☐ Yes ☐ No

23. DOES JD AND COKE, JIMMY AND COKE, OR DARK & STORMY FIT INTO YOUR GENERAL DRINKING PATTERN?

☐ Yes ☐ No

24. DO YOU HAVE CHILDREN WITH MORE THAN TWO PEOPLE?

☐ Yes ☐ No

25. ARE YOUR FAVOURITE COLOURS GREEN AND GOLD?

☐ Yes ☐ No

26. HAVE YOU EVER VOMITED ON AUSTRALIA DAY? ☐ Yes ☐ No

27. DO YOU OWN SKINNY JEANS OR FLANNELETTE CLOTHING? ☐ Yes ☐ No

28. DO YOU KNOW WHAT A V8 SUPERCAR IS? ☐ Yes ☐ No

29. HAVE YOU BEEN SHOPPING IN YOUR PYJAMAS? ☐ Yes ☐ No

30. DO YOU EAT FISH AND CHIPS WITH YOUR FINGERS? ☐ Yes ☐ No

31. DO YOU EAT MEALS IN FRONT OF THE TV? ☐ Yes ☐ No

32. HAVE YOU EVER SAT IN YOUR FRONT GARDEN AND FINISHED A CASE OF BEER? ☐ Yes ☐ No

33. DO YOU EVER SWIG STRAIGHT OUT OF A BOTTLE OF SPIRITS? ☐ Yes ☐ No

34. HAVE YOU EVER STOLEN A SHOPPING TROLLEY? ☐ Yes ☐ No

35. DO YOU EAT TAKEAWAY MORE THAN THREE TIMES A WEEK? ☐ Yes ☐ No

36. **DO YOU KNOW A WAYNE, TRACEY, SHARON, BARRY OR DAZZA?**

Yes No

37. **HAVE YOU EVER GROWN A REALLY LONG GOATEE?**

Yes No

38. **HAVE YOU EVER BEEN HOSPITALISED DUE TO DRUNKEN SHENANIGANS?**

Yes No

39. **ARE YOU NAMED AFTER A MOTOR VEHICLE OR FASHION LABEL E.G. MERCEDES, HARLEY, CHANEL?**

Yes No

40. **IS THERE A BATHTUB, WASHING MACHINE OR COUCH IN YOUR BACKYARD?**

Yes No

41. **HAVE YOU APPEARED ON *A CURRENT AFFAIR* AS A 'NEIGHBOUR FROM HELL'?**

Yes No

42. **HAVE YOU SPENT MORE MONEY DOING UP YOUR CAR THAN WHAT YOU PAID FOR IT?**

Yes No

43. HAVE YOU EVER BREWED YOUR OWN BEER?

☐ Yes ☐ No

44. HAVE YOU EVER BEEN ARRESTED WITHOUT A SHIRT ON?

☐ Yes ☐ No

45. ARE YOU A COLLINGWOOD SUPPORTER?

☐ Yes ☐ No

46. HAVE YOU EVER WORN THE AUSTRALIAN FLAG AS A CAPE?

☐ Yes ☐ No

47. DO YOU LIKE TO WALK THROUGH TRAIN CARRIAGES?

☐ Yes ☐ No

IF YOU ANSWERED YES TO 5–10 QUESTIONS, YOU ARE MILDLY BOGAN.

IF YOU ANSWERED YES TO 11–20 QUESTIONS, YOU'RE SEMI-BOGAN.

IF YOU ANSWERED YES TO 21+ QUESTIONS, YOU ARE LIVING THE BOGAN LIFE IN ALL ITS GLORY AND ARE TO BE CONGRATULATED.

AFTERWORD

Thank you for reading. I hope this guide to the world within
our suburbs and states has opened your eyes and hearts. The next
time you smell sausages overcooked on a BBQ, the next time you
hear a burnout down your street at 3am, think of this beautiful
all-Australian species, the Bogan.

In a world of globalisation, individual anti-authoritarians
are becoming rare. Love the Bogan, they will speak their mind.
Love the Bogan, they will be outrageous in a tamed world. Love the
Bogan, they aren't afraid to be the life of the party! But mostly,
love the Bogan – 'cos they are 110% Australian.

ACKNOWLEDGEMENTS

Thanks to:

BENNY BOGAN & family

VANESSA 'V STAR' DAVIS – hottest ass in NSW

MATT BOWIE – king of the Bogan wranglers

ANGUS FONTAINE – puts the pub in publisher

GINO CAMPAGNARO – shit-hot designer

REBECCA HAMILTON – editor extraordinaire

LUCY INGLIS – media wrangler

ANDREW TAYLOR – agent to the stars

CAST OF HOUSOS

DARREN WILLIAMS

WES BOYD

And all the great Bogans who contributed to this book.
Special thanks to the last of the True Blue Bogans –
you know who you are!